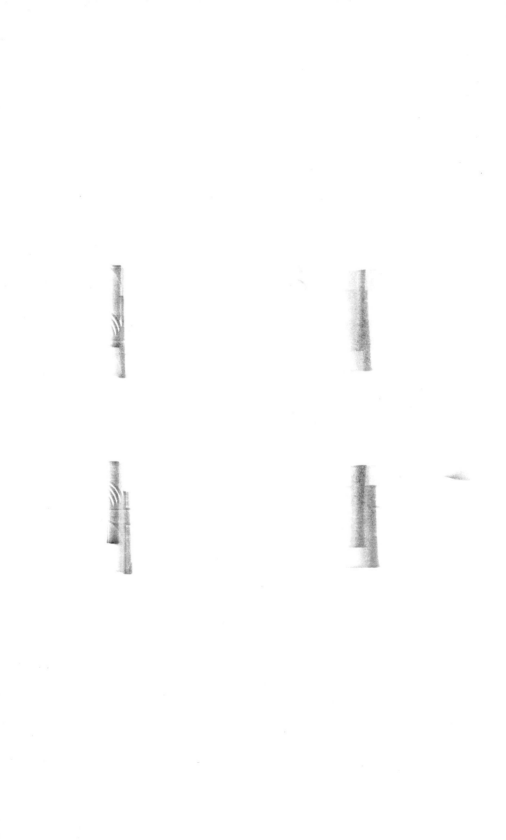

Goodbye to the Orchard

Also by Steven Cramer

Dialogue for the Left and Right Hand (1997)
The World Book (1992)
The Eye That Desires to Look Upward (1987)

Goodbye to the Orchard

POEMS

Steven Cramer

Sarabande Books
LOUISVILLE, KENTUCKY

Managing Editor
Sarabande Books, Inc.
2234 Dundee Road, Suite 200
Louisville, KY 40205

Library of Congress Cataloging-in-Publication Data

Cramer, Steven, 1953–
    Goodbye to the orchard : poems / by Steven Cramer.— 1st ed.
        p.   cm.
    ISBN 1-932511-04-0 (alk. paper) — ISBN 1-932511-05-9 (pbk. : alk. paper)
    1. Loss (Psychology)—Poetry. I. Title.
    PS3553.R2676G66 2004
    811'.54—dc22   2003026023

Cover image: *Vixen,* by Maurice Sendak. Provided courtesy of the artist.

Cover and text design by Charles Casey Martin

Manufactured in Canada
This book is printed on acid-free paper.

Sarabande Books is a nonprofit literary organization.

Partial funding has been provided by the Kentucky Arts Council,
a state agency in the Commerce Cabinet, with support from the
National Endowment for the Arts.

FIRST EDITION

To Hilary, Charlotte, and Ethan

And in memory of Mary Anne Cramer (1952–2001)

Contents

Acknowledgments

My thanks to the editors of the following periodicals, in which some of these poems, or earlier versions of them, originally appeared:

AGNI: "A Basket of Eggs," "Harm," "It Is Night in My Study," "Morning Walk in the Orchard," "Phantom Pain"

The Atlantic Monthly: "Everyone Who Left Us"

The Boston Phoenix: "From a Letter"

Crab Orchard Review: "Prinsengracht 236"

Flyway: "The Toughest Thing"

The Greensboro Review: "Lack," "Queequeg's Ramadan"

Harvard Review: "Lunch at the Underground," "That'll Be the Day"

Indiana Review: "Life and Death," "Nice"

The Journal: "Bipolar"

The Kenyon Review: "Miracle Gro"

The Paris Review: "The House Once Identified as Paradise," "Of Late," "Starting and Ending with Sade"

Partisan Review: "Throw Yourself Like Seed"

Ploughshares: "Goodbye to the Orchard"

Poetry: "Draft of a Dream," "Singer," "Sixties Couple, the Haight"

Salamander: "After a Phrase by József," "Long Distance," "Partial Glance, Through the *O.E.D.*'s Magnifying Glass, at 'Thing'"

Slate: "At Shining Rock," "Body on the Brain," "The Dread Museum," "Word Gets Around"

Tarpaulin Sky: "Maurice," "Progressive"

West Branch: "Late Quartet," "The Soul"

With love and gratitude: Teresa Cader, Gail Mazur, Roland Merullo, Joyce Peseroff, Robert Pinsky, Hilary Rao, Maurice Sendak, Sue Standing, Thomas Swiss.

Special thanks to David Rivard
for his suggestions on organizing this book.

With hey, ho, the wind and the rain...
For the rain it raineth every day.

       —Twelfth Night

With hey, ho, the wind and the rain...
Though the rain it raineth every day.

        —King Lear

THROW YOURSELF LIKE SEED

after Miguel de Unamuno

Defeat? Shake it off, take yourself back. Lying
in bed, sheet over your eyes, you'll miss the wheel
that grazes your heel as it passes by, turning—
whoever wants to live has some life left.

Right now, you're just feeding yourself
with a mortal pain that spins its web inside you;
life equals work, and work is the single
lasting thing; get started; turn back to the work.

Throw yourself like seed as you walk your field,
don't turn this way or that; that's turning toward death;
don't let what happened slow you. What's alive

in the furrow, let it live; what's inside you, let die.
Nobody's life drifts by like a landscape with clouds;
the day you collect yourself is the day you work.

I

BIPOLAR

Just after the downpour moves on, and it's
still a swamp of viridian and emerald
indoors and out; and the central power grid,
iffy at best, still sputters and spits;

and the citizens, alert, still hunch
by their wavering flames, tensed for the flinch
between each white shock and its thunderclap
(relaxing, a bit, as quiet widens the gap)—

it's then this German-folktale kind of calm
seeps in: brown of the briar rose, a bone-
meal wariness, the green tone of *once upon
a time, a woodman and his wife wanted children*—

and soon children came. That's the time
to pray whoever loves you escaped harm.

THE HOUSE ONCE IDENTIFIED AS PARADISE:

never receives visitors, only inhabitants.
Outside, icicles thaw from the eaves in winter,
and even with its windows painted shut,
a spring smell persists. That's normal, yes,
despite this ambiguity: Are those roses
on the wallpaper or menstrual stains? Only here
can women spit as skillfully as men, and men
emote so freely. Try living up to the house
once identified as paradise. Try and fail.

Once identified as paradise, the house
loses interest for some. How can you walk
down a hallway so narrow you must hold hands?
What's the good of a bedroom without regret,
a kitchen with no promise of violence,
guiltless parlors? Starlings chatter in the elms,
as if to sing the sweetness of the garden and grounds.
The gods, capricious and cruel, or reliable
and cruel, spread their beneficence and gossip.
Still, from dirt roads and dirtier sidewalks,

from orphanages, from the dead, we come to the house.
Those others, however, the holdouts, take strength
from the root of *enemy*, not only damned but wrong.

We're loyal, empty-handed; we know we're lost.
We know the women we long to bed will marry us,
that the men, oh lucky men!, won't resist love.
That we'll ascend because we've always ascended—
in early autumn, when apples hail down on the roof,
in late autumn, when the orchard reeks of vinegar.

MORNING WALK IN THE ORCHARD

Can't remember what I must have wanted,
or if it was worth losing, but I sure
feel it burn my skin, as in the dream
when my best friend told me not to touch
my best friend. Now all that's left
is my flat look back, the mist
burning off Mount Anthony by ten,
a haze of gnats nagging at my head—
the sun here, the sun there, promising
another day to spoil. What's the look

the world gives back, if not
this paper wasp, hang-gliding, silent,
lighting on a stalk of goldenrod
then swerving off to chew wood pulp
or hover into someone's outdoor seminar,
the lit professor's polysyllables
turned to squeals. Nice going, wasp.
And the gate to the so-called Secret Garden,
left ajar, moans in a breeze that's sure
to die down by late afternoon. So

even if that something lost was lovely,
cool-skinned, and like the dew on stones
in the still-damp ground, disappearing,

there's a way not to wander, but to walk
on the ground without embarrassment.
Yes, it was sweet, a little weedy too.
I take the time to wish it back, then let
the mind say, as it always will, *Come in,
come in; it's getting too hot to stay out.*

THE TOUGHEST THING

De Kooning said paint is flesh
but confessed his women baffled him.
This morning you shrugged on my denim shirt
then shrugged it off and put it on again.
Your belly, rounded but not yet round,
made you stand a little ducklike in
your underpants. Then you squeezed past me

and the door closed behind you like the last page
of a brochure about amniocentesis, designed
to frighten us, which it did, and afterward
the week you planned to go away
began. I don't plan to get any better
at going without you. Remember
the lunches, the kiss in the right place?

Ten years and the toughest thing so far
was when you gave up eating anything
that had swallowed, known sex, given birth.
The worst? Those piles of sliced cucumber—
the circumference of each disk fringed
by scraping a fork down the sides
of the peeled, whole thing.

Here are some Perdue chicken tenders;
here are the cluster tomatoes that tasted
like pumpkins, and therefore foretold Charlotte;
and here, in the Cheerios, is the nasal *R*
in "you're still here," and the long *O*
of the throes of labor, and all
the small o's in the milk. The whole milk.

LACK

on being asked to define it

On the one hand, it's the look
of snow if you haven't seen snow,
a chill behind the curved bone
of the forehead when you can't
sleep, and yet some kind
of self-love lasts the night.

Same hand still, I'll go out
on this limb: befriended,
it makes life worth it, as long
as we don't expect we'll be
reborn. On the other hand,
probably the left, my best

shot in the dark is this:
if every number's negative;
a glove's a hardened fist;
desire amounts to a thrust,
lost nerve, an antidepressant
sealed in gelatin; then

lack is a place not so much
brisk as windblown, where
what's wrong really is wrong
in the story. Then our faces

sting from the wet of its kiss
whenever we walk into it—

as if across a February
heath, feet testing for ice
with each new step along
the hardening ground, wind
bending the treetops so distant
they register at first as smoke.

QUEEQUEG'S RAMADAN

Chiming/unchiming
the wind chime, it's the
                            wind again.
It can sing, it can riffle through
Melville, it can clear
its throat in the wake of a sneeze
coming from the one not yet one year
(call him Ethan)

for whom most everything's meditation: the swallow-
tail caterpillar,
"ants
worshipping a toad-stool,"
the spun cocoon & the built dam,

or this October day so circumspect
I can hear a neighbor tear aluminum foil
& a Bell Atlantic lineman linking
            someone to the Web—
            Phillips head in his grip & if
I project it so, perilously close to his eye . . .

Forgive me, Ethan.
I've got a squid's habit for spewing black.

Life's not all orange juice
& wet Labradors, though your life,
        it's true enough,
        began in the groin
or a gland not far behind it, & true
enough is enough truth, lest we forget
Queequeg's Ramadan—

how he crouched on his hams,
cool as a graven idol, balancing
        little Yojo on his head—& how
        meditation & water never go
where we will them to go, but will
where we want them to, or so goes
the plumber's mantra. Therefore,

        sing, Mr. Biblical, sing
        that ole Devile, the sea.

"We're terribly cracked about the head
        & sadly in need of mending."

BODY ON THE BRAIN

When the larva hit the omelet pan,
curling, warping, maybe even
sizzling a bit, I wanted more
data to connect my ruined home-
fries to the moths I'd been applauding
all summer into dust. But when
I saw its kin threading up the collar
of the Colavita Extra Virgin Olive Oil,
I scrubbed the cupboards with all
the Formula 409 to be found, finding
larvae in the flour, in the corn
meal last used in the late eighties,
the creamy-style Skippy, the Basmati rice,
the sesame seeds and Aunt Jemima Lite.
I swabbed, I purged. I itched
the way I'm itching now to get this right
so you'll scratch too. Do you
believe your body merely feels
when it blinks and recoils, figuring
it may have eaten grubs, or do
you think, as Freud did, that each
twitch or catch in the throat
constitutes a thought? I marvel
how the body we're wired to adore
disgusts us when we cast it

out into the world. Spit
repeatedly into a juice glass, drink it.
Every day you drink a hundred times
this half-cup of saliva. We get
our lessons in otherness where we can.
How else could I stare into the porridge
of my daughter's diarrhea, swallowing
hard to keep from adding to it, yet grateful
she's still mine enough to let me check?
Or when we add our stink to a stranger's
stink from the next stall, two stinks
stink less than one—and isn't this
how mind and body mate when we're in love?

THE SOUL

The self, only more so, it is said.
Some say *round*; some say, *won't float.*
Not even a mammal, far as I know.

Burton divided it into three parts:
the *Vegetable*, which borrows its heat
from digestion, and tends toward light;

the *Animal-Sensible* saves what's seen—
as wax doth the imprint of a seal—then
shades the seen into dreams; the *Rational*

talks with angels, or strives to, divining
their breath on our mirrors. Like us,
then, the soul without names proves

mythic as the roc's nest. Like me!—
along with my instinct to herd my kids
to the lawn-edge of sidewalks, or to lean

into their manners of play: lips pursed,
clerical, over their coloring; those ticklish,
breakable collarbones. How they terrify me.

A NIGHT TERROR

They weren't cries rising from Ethan's crib,
but wet shrieks we wakened to, sobs for air.
His neck a loose hinge, I held him in terror.
Hilary, two fingers down his throat, probed:

nothing. Pupils scanning us, discovering
nothing too, where the floor and doorjamb met
he rocked, flooded, refusing juice or comfort.
Meanwhile, *autistic* added to our throng

of sickening scare-words, we considered
a slap to bring him back, then a video,
and chose the video. Two episodes
found his point of sleep on Hilary's ribs,

and next morning how his human eyes peered
at ours, like ours, beat being eyed by God.

DRAFT OF A DREAM

The message I found on the post-it note
went thus: *love truth; expect to be found out.*
Kid-style capitals proved I wrote it, but
left no clue why I'd swelled into a fat

clause no editor could edit; then, an entry
on a shrink's list of patient slang for sex—
her desk Norwegian teak, the mug of tea
on which she had affixed *her* post-it notes

hot against her knuckle, their lips of stickum
loosening... And yet, I knew the note
to peel away at hour's end would terminate
our sessions—cool as the draft her linen

skirt was lifting to: *Love, just stay benighted,*
given everything I know you've got to hide.

PROGRESSIVE

From now on, simply aim your nose
at whatever you wish to see clearly,
said the optician. Aiming his nose at me,

he fitted new frames to my temples
then sketched the concept of progressives:
two circles with an hourglass in each,

the lower field for literature, life on top.
Some of what he didn't say includes:
floors constantly awash as if rain-swept;

late-day dumbness, mid-skull; an urge to tuck
my head into my chest, doubling my chin—
each a glimpse of unhurried mortality,

the ghost in the corner of the eye.
Reading a long-lined poem, I've found
I must shake my head slightly, the way

we listen to a friend's tale of woe or weal
(broken timing-belt, biopsy finally benign),
empathy shading to impatience, with a mote

of regret at how rarely we're actually tragic
or even tragicomic, as in the Fool's riddle
to Lear: *thou canst tell why one's nose stands*

i' th' middle on's face? As for Lear,
knucklehead this joke's meant to instruct,
he learns, too late, *it's to keep one's eyes*

of either side's nose, that what a man cannot
smell out, he may spy into. As for me,
it's early yet: will the pupils adjust,

and vision grow indivisible again?
As for my reading, for now I'll stick
with wheelbarrow-era Williams, or Oppen,

anything with more depth than width.
I'll practice keeping an eye on me later:
searching for my glasses, or the receipt

required for the rebate on the frames—
even down on my knees, nosing around
the garbage, always the last place we look.

GOODBYE TO THE ORCHARD

Beautiful from the get-go, we were
incarnations of the new, and pure sex.
I'll miss that, along with the unicorns.
The organic bower of our garden grew
into anybody's memory of a bed
or a mattress, in a shack near a lake.
"Mistakes, like love, are to be *made*,"
you said. I hadn't thought of that.

That first autumn was easy, the liquor
of decay headiest at noon. And the orchard,
let's face it, had begun to resemble a casino,
all its tables rigged in our favor. The yoke
of being cared for is what cast us out,
not that immense, bearded librarian,
our curator, and not our having learned
how to get on one another's nerves.

Goodbye to the orchard: green
one day, the next day blood. We know
to stiffen at a voice; how to tell the truth
from an untruth; what's sweet, what stinks.
Behind each sleeping dog, another to let lie.

Who knew an innocence taking ages to perfect
could fall so short when time came to live?
You knew, and then you let me know.

SINGER

I knew trouble and endured it,
grief and desire my companions.
In winter my enemy attacked.
The better of the two, I was bound
in rope made from my own sinew.
All that has passed, and so may this.

There was a man condemned to live
outside the city he loved—even death
meant less in exile—and a woman
who dreaded the child inside her.
Her dreams were dreams of drowning.
All that has passed, and so may this.

If the mind becomes a wolf's mind,
it will force misery on misery,
make cowards heroes. If courtiers
want the kingdom overthrown, yet fail
to speak, they will remain courtiers.
All that has passed, and so may this.

At first doom sees, wherever it turns,
more doom. Then, in time: joy.
I'll say this about myself: my name

was a name you knew, and I sang
until another singer took my place.
All that has passed, and so will this.

After the Anglo-Saxon poem, "Deor"

II

NICE:

Chiefly British, it can mean *delicious*, as when Greg refers to a *nice mince pie*. He means the opposite of the *awful pie* in "Dockery and Son," where Larkin says: *life is first boredom, then fear*—after changing trains in the furnace-fumes of Sheffield, the city where I spent my "junior year abroad" and first met Greg, among the better men I know.

Greg used *nice* for the sauces, puddings, sausages, and peas hefted onto our plates at the truckers' café three blocks from the University. It catered mainly to students who, said the women serving us, were *ducks*—as in: *What you having, ducks?*—and sometimes *doves*. From Greg I learned to use my knife to plow food onto the back of my fork—an English-style avidity Keats called *gusto*.

Visiting Keats's Hampstead house with Greg two summers ago, apart from a twitch in my spine while staring at the lock of hair, what I remember best is how nicely London alerts you to speed bumps coming up: *bumps for half a mile*, as well as the Yorkshire lorry driver who hoisted Greg and me out of the sooty Sheffield rain nearly three decades before, addressing each of us as *luv*, without embarrassment, all the way to London. *Nice*—

as in *kind, considerate to others*, like Dan and Isobel, Greg and Gill's teenagers, playing the word game "sausages" with Charlotte and Ethan; the eight of us packed into their minivan; cows and full-grown lambs like sponged paint on the Kentish hillsides; Greg and I attempting "The General Prologue" and getting no further than *from every shires ende/Of Engelond to Canterbury they wende;* Hilary and Gill doing most of the driving. A day when almost every word, said or unsaid, seemed benign....

In Chaucer's time, *nice* could also mean *foolish.* Which may be why, in our day, the tough-minded deplore it. If someone described a poem as *nice,* we'd think *insipid,* wouldn't we?—as in: *thin,* like those astonishingly narrow English beds I never got used to sleeping in. This evening, though, with its summer air damp after rain; my back lawn and its bordering woods greening what's left of the light, I'll take *nice.* And I'll take *benign* over *malignant*—because, once dying became more tedious than frightening, her hospice bed broadening as she shrank, my sister called the taste of tapioca *nice,* and *nice* the smell of the roast beef she couldn't eat. Sometimes we ate her meals as she slept, so they wouldn't go to waste.

MIRACLE GRO

I was finishing one book about ghosts
and about to start another about ghosts
while she slept. "If life is ordinary,
so is death," our sister (soon *my* sister) told me

between books, then offered her solution
for my pitiful, languishing garden—
its tomatoes oozing a thin, black blood,
its shrunken peppers, with their stunted heads:

Miracle Gro and water, but not from the tap.
Our sister, our dying one.... Looking up,
we watched the March light she was lying in,
unseasonably green, through the hospice window,

warm even for the South—and hatefully so,
to one who's never been much good with soil.

LIFE AND DEATH

More and more, and never enough, gets said:
in the debates between specialist and priest;
the histories of Purgatory; *The New*

Oxford Treasury of Death-Bed Wit;
and even in our elegies to pets—
the bubble-eyed goldfish and twin dwarf frogs

dead on the ninth, the first, the twenty-first,
our daughter waking to their buoyant
corpses belly-up in her aquarium,

its water wheel still filtering the water
weeks afterward. The wash upon wash
of her chemo over, my sister and Joe

made a video of their marriage vows,
the garden center girl assuring us
a crape myrtle *FTD*'d to their wedding

would give lavender and white blossoms
quickly in southern soil and light. Yet
her mucinous tumor took its time, regrew

according to death's nature, which is
to defeat what music we make out of it:
I can no more delays devise, but welcome

pain, let pleasure pass. . . . The delays devised
today can go marrow-deep, like the stem-
cell transplant Don, our hard friend, came close

to dying of, coming back softer-tongued—
"lymphoma-free," he says, "four years running
and counting on my five-year milestone."

So maybe waiting's all a life counts on,
the way we waited, years ago, as Don rowed
our daughter out across Lake Shaftsbury.

Their boat shrinking to a glimmering dot,
we tensed at any shout, or shift of wind,
until he doubled back and docked, the sun

a too-white bright on his skin, yet milder
than the glare of hospice light she peered through,
the month my sister gave up food, then water.

"I'll see you soon," aimed at her sedated eyes,
came the closest I could to goodbye, plus
one valedictory kiss. Backing out,

I watched her hands lift, take my hands.
Two kisses, she instructed, even though
she'd hardly breathed a syllable all day.

And once my lips quit the flaking gray
tissue of her lips, *three more*, she ordered.
In a week, blinking twice at Joe, she left us

no more care to volunteer; no crying
quarantined to the lounge; no rib by rib
massages until she slept; no more waking

to stomach bile refluxed into a pail;
no more delirious, gnomic sayings:
I know somebody, now, who knows I am;

and no more speculation, as when I said
"maybe it's just a better childhood—this life
after death, I mean," not sure she'd heard. And her:

I think my afterlife will be smooth sailing
in your memory . . . Which brought us back, then,
to the ferry ride across the Chesapeake

we each remembered differently, and yet
alike enough: a foghorn, and therefore fog;
real dolphins, pacing us, portside; and lifting

each of us, in turn, to the rail for a view,
who other than our father?—sober, sane,
alive, or at least that's how he looked to us.

AT SHINING ROCK

More certain she was dying now,
she tried new ways to speak:
comical yet grim, like the wig
she'd thumbed down, preferring
earth-toned scarves, and irony
the color of her I.V. bruise.
Too late, I've learned I'm the life
of my own party—this said,
walking the dog, *to* the dog.

On days when she felt curious,
she pictured the rogue cells
aswarm in her lower bowel
as colonies of mold on bread.
Other days she had us labeling
her belongings with our names—
paperbacks first, then hardcovers,
the contents of a brass jewelry box,
mutually grooming horses on its lid.

Sometimes such preparedness
struck us as a kind of mania:
I'm terrified, she said, *but never felt*
such joy, taking her pocket *Psalms*
to the back porch to perform 121—

her congregation, twenty seedlings
in twenty milk cartons of soil.
In a late-May rainfall, she led us
up the muddy slope to Shining Rock.

White oak, as we rose, gave into
mountain ash, scrub, veined granite.
Scatter me anywhere around here,
she said, offering her psalm again:
I lift my eyes to the hills, from whence . . .
To feel the wind and rain abating
as she read, deciduous and pine
making miles of uniform green,
you must stand still, still as she stood.

EVERYONE WHO LEFT US

Everyone who left us we find everywhere.
It's easier, now, to look them in the eyes—
At gravesites, in bed, when the phone rings.
Of course, we wonder if they think of us.

It's easier, now, to look them in the eyes,
Imagine touching a hand, listening to them talk.
Of course, we wonder if they think of us
When nights, like tonight, turn salty, warm.

Imagine touching a hand, listening to them talk—
Hard to believe they're capable of such coldness.
When nights, like tonight, turn salty, warm,
We think of calling them, leaving messages.

Hard to believe they're capable of such coldness—
No color, no pulse, not even a nerve reaction.
We think of calling them, leaving messages
Vivid with news we're sure they'd want to know.

No color, no pulse, not even a nerve reaction:
We close our eyes in order not to see them.
Vivid with news, we're sure they'd want to know
We don't blame them, really. They weren't cruel.

We close our eyes in order not to see them
Reading, making love, or falling asleep.
We don't blame them. Really, they weren't cruel,
Though it hurts every time we think of them:

Reading, making love, or falling asleep,
Enjoying the usual pleasures and boredoms.
Though it hurts every time we think of them,
Like a taste we can't swallow their names stay.

Enjoying the usual pleasures and boredoms,
Then, they leave us the look of their faces
Like a taste we can't swallow. Their names stay,
Diminishing our own, getting in the way

At gravesites, in bed, when the phone rings.
Everyone who left us we find everywhere,
Then they leave us, the look of their faces
Diminishing, our own getting in the way.

PARTIAL GLANCE, THROUGH THE O.E.D.'S MAGNIFYING GLASS, AT "THING"

for Robert Pinsky

Before English was English, "an assembly
or parliament," in which our wrinkled kings
collected in the sagas of their power;

but also, by Elizabeth's reign, both common
cock and cunt; and thus, the four monoliths
at the State Government Mall in Albany,

their marble facings more like white formica—
how could they build such things?—and the pits
their piles were driven into, to erect

places to make Speer's stadiums look delicate;
but also the slaves of Michelangelo,
forever lugging the marble of themselves

to the tomb of Julius II—*poor things,*
a Ghanian student said, and then explained
the thing or two those Krobo chieftains knew

who stayed rich as "palm-oil kings,"
once the Dutch abolished trade in slaves;
and thus, our brands of cold thrift; but also

the cool utility of our Teflon
spatulas, and micro-threads of Polypro:
sheer, sweat-free skins we shed after exercise

in bedrooms like the one, on *This Old House*,
made nautical with a father's fishing nets:
things personal, then, compared to *property*

real, according to English law—the first
defining my sister's ashes and bone bits,
the second, her living and legal wills clipped

from *Consumer Reports* (every mandate,
from *advance directives* to her *power
of attorney*, a box to check, or to leave

blank), as well as the pewter urn we bought
to replace the box her remains came in,
yet we agreed to keep the box; and thus

any amulet, of rock or shell or paper,
like the letters we stored, yet still can't read,
in a plastic milk crate, the space they take

a thing pitiably small as the smallest boy
ever to wear an Eton jacket; but also
"Eton" as an emblem, which signifies

the power to select some, and others
to reject: *select/reject* a near-true rhyme;
and thus, word-chains chiming but not meaning

to explain: *a triangle has three sides,*
and there's nothing you can do about it—
or word-chains meaning to: *no tattoo's*

a thing of joy forever—the first one Zen,
the second John Waters, the theme he spoke on,
All Flesh Sags, so true we wrinkled and howled;

but also, the hospice doctor's whispering,
kneeling by my sister's bed, both of them
something to see, so we looked, and saw

a doctor appearing to pray; and thus
my sister's cause, though lost, still a case
to plead, like Cordelia's *no cause no cause*

lifting up her king of inches and patches,
but as her father, freshly clothed, who kneels
to her and sees and knows her; but also,

at last, this magnifying glass my breath
has misted over, and through which I've looked
and looked and looked, till I can barely see

a thing; and thus, a last scene's final prop—
the looking-glass, placed near Cordelia's lips,
which seems to cloud, although it doesn't cloud.

FROM A LETTER

Chincoteague Island

Behind the cypresses, the ponies
keep their distance. They bite and kick
when someone tries to feed them.

I come here when I want to feel
a little less like dying. "Dire cure," yes—
what I eat tastes like what I've digested.

After all the tests, my Buddhist friend
said "rocks fall." That hurt. I liked it.
Cancer makes you stop, of course.

Snow geese whitening a pond, a family
of marsh wrens: these have helped some.
Now my chemo's over, for the time being,

I think a circle is the perfect shape.
When beach grass draws a ring around itself,
it's just a trick of the wind, but

I see Jesus sketching O's in the sand.
I see him crouch and bide his time.
It's crazy: knowing what will kill me,

I still get angry if the mail comes late.
Strange phrase, "the time being."

III

WILL WE EVER FIND A PLANET LIKE OUR OWN?

That is, this cobble with the fire inside it,
its infinite coroners, its black and white
back lots, hosts of the hooded and unsung
and the proud flesh required of their young?—

where, however harebrained it gets to say
great to be alive, however literal
the ichor of the gods becomes (until
it's a mustard-colored discharge from the eye);

there's still a child's riveting mistake
to see the moon's not full but "fixed," his *lookit*
exhaled, a cloud of awe, last January;
and the sweet ignorance to wonder *why*

are all their faces smiling? of obit
upon obit upon obit upon obit.

HARM

Love means nothing if it does not mean
loving some more than others, Orwell said—
in his hatred of saints a hero of mine.
And this is how it is with love:

before he'd write "A Hanging,"
he spent months trying to describe light
angling through his blinds. And one day
he did. Over the next few days,

reading *The Winter's Tale* again,
I'll try and fail to keep my daughter
from replays of the soccer jersey billowing
as a boy drops into the SWAT team's arms,

two bullets in his brain. So afraid
of throwing up she only plays at home,
she trusts, at best, the germlessness
between the moment

she strips the wrapper off a straw
and the moment she puts it to her lips.
When hungry, she calls hunger
the belt that hurts her waist, thirst

a space that turns blue-green,
the color she loves best. Of the boy
who fell from the library window,
"he'll survive," I tell her. And he does,

unlike Mamillius, who whispers now
his sad tale that's best for winter
into his mother's ear, a secret we take
to be this play of jealousy itself,

which kills them both offstage,
only to revive Hermione, but not her child.
That's the harm the play won't heal,
even as she wakes from stone, and walks

down to us; even as I overhear
my daughter whisper to her playdate,
sleep still unsettling her voice: *last night*
I didn't dream one dream. It was just black.

THE DREAD MUSEUM

Another plane, flames inside, gone down—
fundamentalist genius for terror, or just
an apolitical mechanical malfunction,
no one knows. Not the aeronautics
or explosive experts; not the anchors
paid too much to tell us; and most
terribly, not the relatives who watch
On Time switch to *Canceled* on the monitors.

Maybe it was too much picturing—
the sheared wing thrust from the sea,
torsos afloat like hand puppets in a tub,
the grim business of the divers, nosing through
the ribs of Business and Coach—that brought on
this nosebleed hampering me all morning.
Can't bend, can't yawn, can't make a face
without my nostril-wad Kleenex reddening.

Amazing—isn't it?—how one swerves
from pity for bodies and body parts to hordes
of corpuscles and antibodies surging.
Should I be ashamed? I'm not. And I'm not
that I'm relieved I'm not, once again,
the relative reaching over the butcherblock
for the telephone, and in that lurch

having the notion common to us all—
now's my time to pay for pleasure—
prove true.
             Oh, I could weep
out of frustration for my nose, and may.
I'll put my head back, daub a few last drops
on another bloody lucky day, and dwell
on the wheels, on the spokes of the wheels,
of my daughter's tricycle, while someone
whom I'll never meet and care about
as much as care imagined can, tears out
the front-page photo of a size-4 Nike
washed ashore, because he knows
he knows the shoe.

OF LATE

By year's end, some couples used book lights,
or even night lights, so as not to make love
in total dark. What some told, others took in
with the hungry curiosity of three-year-olds
ripping open gifts. Story after story

jutted up like fossil finds, tinted rose
by sun and smoke and dust, the air space
silenced, through which innocence strained
like a grammar-school string orchestra.

With time, we'll learn again not to curse
on camera; in time, we'll identify one another.
For now, "one" often makes "another" jump—
appearing, say, at the cellar door, in one hand
something sharp and gleaming from the tool-kit.

PRINSENGRACHT 263

When the bookcase that concealed steps
leading to the top-floor annex opened—
like a false wall from *Hold That Ghost*—
sweat passed from your hand into mine.
When we saw the posters in her bedroom
of Gable, Lombard, even Rin-Tin-Tin,
we'd seen enough. Until we ran
into a party of German girls, flown in
from *Gymnasium* to single-file, so it
seemed, through collective guilt. Looking
out the window she looked out of,
we almost hated them; no, did. Who
were we to wish these teens gave more
than a shit about history; and anyway,
poetry should be oblique,
right?
        Okay. Amsterdam
struck us every day as quaint, small-
minded, too pretty to take seriously.
The gabled houses appeared to bow
and brandish all four ornamental types—
the step, the spout, the neck, the bell.
Pulleys hoisted pianos and hope chests.
The bile-green murk of the *grachts*
turned lovely if the surface caught

the houseboat lights just right. Yes—
we had a few good evening walks.
I'd found a reliable laundry, the best
market for fresh fruit; I knew my way...
Those tourist girls drummed their thumbs
on the glass over her report cards;
they giggled, jostled, poked, trading
rich stupidities anyone who has lived
through adolescence knows. How easily
she'd have jostled, poked, and giggled back.

A BASKET OF EGGS

The rill of blood from rib to thigh; tendons
stretched taut, gravity's ache straining through;
flesh the weathered ochre of exhumed bone—
Brunelleschi's Christ shook Donatello so,

he dropped his basket of eggs. Eras later,
outside Santa Maria Novella,
a nursing mother's breast turned sootier
with each step we took, her day's pool of lira

collecting in her skirt-lap, flies on the orbits
of her infant's eyes. Sights from a honeymoon,
reposited in memory—like our coin
after coin to light the angels, saints, lunettes—

along with the noise of *Christ, eggs, soot, flies,*
and the wing-brush of skirts across stone floors.

STARTING AND ENDING WITH SADE

I am not happy, but I'm well: enough
to suppose an unmedicated mind
a clean one. Not *washed*—like those elective
amputees, or "wannabes," who'll lose a limb

on their homemade guillotines, for a mean
feeling of completion, and then tie off
their stumps with a washcloth, dialing 911.
No, not washed, but *buffed,* for the body's rebirth,

all its holes aglow, wrote Sade, or should have.
Patron saint of the mouth choiring *mine,*
his arch cranium, ripped off from his grave,
showed not one erotic bump or dent. So clean

a skull, much like a priest's, it rests assured:
pleasure is always weakened, when it's shared.

PHANTOM PAIN

Whatever made her want to do it—
or whoever—she's not sure;
but she wants to do it more
deeply these days. The first time

felt accidental: a shift
in their typical skin-to-skin relation,
her body arching like a question
he answered with his body

in this new way. Now she can't tell
if it's hunger for shame
or a means to overthrow
whoever took her, night after night,

into the cellar-dark humidity
she never completely remembers
except in ways the body remembers:
a sore on her lip, a red patch

on her tongue if she talks too much
about it. The next time scared her.
She felt a hand cup her belly
and lift her. Not his hand, or hers,

and not the hand of a stranger.
When he guided himself in,
she trusted him, encouraged him
to follow her. Wet as he was

in the sweat of his good luck,
she could never tell him his cock
was anybody's cock—at best
a thing to ride till something gave.

The third time seemed to last
much of the night. That it felt good
frightened her even more, as if
pleasure were always part gift, part

violation. When they ended this time,
the original urge was gone and
not gone, like the lost limb
amputees report, first

as an itch, and then
an impossible, palpable hurt.

SIXTIES COUPLE, THE HAIGHT

after a photograph by William Gedney

Loosely tucked under army-surplus bedding,
she fondles his two-day shadow with her thumb,
his thumb reaching to tease the D-string
on a Gibson solid-body propped behind them,

as if to urge sustain fluid as Clapton's—
God's that is—or Hendrix's phallic rage.
Next year, once silence takes the election,
they'll forsake their mattress for a marriage

bed, as the Summer of Love these nestlings
embodied in a flash hardens to grist
for riffs like this: which I conceived, at first,
as a love song for you. May I keep being

your suitable alternative to no one,
my interminable solos all forgiven?

for Hilary

LUNCH AT THE UNDERGROUND

"Maybe we're all piano keys
or organ stops," said Dostoyevsky.
We pondered this a moment over lunch:
tofu burgers, black bean salad,
something green and Asian. No one
dared to ask what Fyodor meant.

Then each of us returned to our bouquet
of student themes, every one enticing
as a tax form, the warming trend
awakening a plague of cluster flies.
Emotions? Yes, we had them.

Dozing off in my recliner,
one last thought, and not my best
example of everyday Zen: *if we are*
the instrument he said we were,
what notes should we strike?

"What can you expect," he sighed
at tea, "about this strange creature?
Give him money, cakes, and sleep.
He'll let the cakes rot, and all night
stay up squandering the money,
even if it's only out of spite."

LATE QUARTET

Don't judge him by his marginalia, or mistake
his fresh ideas for stale, as when he'd replicate

the early morning bickering of rival birds
on piccolo and triangle. Remember, instead,

the spirit he spent on exactitude, on students
scattering their tenuto and staccato notes

as if casting grain (or, at their age, like Onan).
That the ass is the sexiest body part—this axiom

he shared with Mozart, though not his genius
to write to Constanze: *I'd shit oranges*

for your kiss. What use has genius for tact?
Recitals to dwindling parlors; slights at court;

oyster-flavored praise from philistines; fever—
these shrink to minor irritants, like nose hair,

when genius strips off its wig, gets it right.
As a dog lies patient for a noon pool of sunlight,

he craved fame, but was passive in pursuing it.
And now he's easier to live with: a draft

found among his scores of drafts, fifty or so
phrases ringing true, yet none quite so true

as the pages, in their blankness, giving sway
to idleness, the start of all psychology.

AFTER A PHRASE BY JÓZSEF

Believe me, Steven, I love you. A lot.
Fess up to it, then: you're not *so* lonely
and unfatherly. As long as gravity
slides hope through the lips of your mail slot;

and rock stars evolve airier guitars;
and the heart, at its most democratic, beats
equally in you and your ruby-crowned kinglets
perched on their swing set, safe from predators—

what persists persists like Vermeer's pearl earring,
crisp as a baked wishbone, or a pressed fern;
yolky as an infant's bangs when born
glistening, mum, wary—a skeptic peering

into the white glare of delivery,
before the nitrate eyewash primes a cry.

LONG DISTANCE

She wouldn't hear of it: "I'm *not* dying
young," forty-nine years being quite enough,
my sister's fibrous voice kept insisting.
Back then, her sentences would taper off

like a child from homework, or like a drunk's
slurred kiss, a trail of liquid soap. My free ear
plugged with my left forefinger, I'd lower
the *Nicktoons* and curse, haplessly, the trucks

on Bedford Street; and still receive these ghost
tones from "the brainy one" to whom I'd given
more than one concussion. If she said *Christ,*
I heard *tests;* and now, though her phone

is disengaged, the voice persists: "I *didn't*
die before my time," if I've heard it right.

THAT'LL BE THE DAY:

the mind finally unwinds its clockwork nights;
and the body calms its restless leg syndrome
wiring calves to thighs—all panic gone
like the *phtt* an opened coffee can emits.

Thereafter, pleasures taken—a hardcover's
heft on the lap; the senses' high five;
how Leonardo's wings and pulleys save
a screen—will rhyme, albeit off, with labors.

Oh earthy clumps kneaded into lamps of clay
a potter's skill can center! Oh, the toys
of thought thought busted! They just need batteries.
I can't help hoping to be with me on that day

when each fat chance, for good, is realized—
the brilliant dying brilliant; the wise, wise.

MAURICE

"For instance, take the art of sitting down.
I've just begun learning how it's done—

the calves and hamstrings tightening,
the balls of the feet accommodating

a few more micrograms of gravity
along the spinal column, the vertebrae

stiffening to hold the trunk upright,
knees unlocking, tendons slackening to let

them bend; then—settling, spreading—the rump
adapting to, adopting, the seat's shape:

mechanics wise as this will take the body
roughly a year to master; but a mind

like mine, apparently, took seventy
to get the sheer sweetness of that wisdom."

WORD GETS AROUND

But Word's not sure what to make of the world.
Forget epic sweep; and, please, not one more
alter-ego sequence. Word wants a new hymn.

This morning's address: the circular wash
of a street sweep's brush, strident jays, brats
on Schwinns, semi's bulked-up like blue whales

whose all-day shiftings and downshiftings
bypass the white noise of Word's window fan.
Every gear-chafing-gear is the cry (if fish

cried) of an eel squished through a sieve.
For the realtor who called Word's address
"a *cul-de-sac* of quietude," let us reserve

a hereafter of such squeals. Yet he can't
just curse out of his cave like a Caliban,
can he?—pawsful of pignuts and filberts,

young scammels from the shallows—
to try and bribe this brave new world?
Aspiring to a wind chime's disinterest,

try as he might, Word can't care less.
He wants to know what's in it: being wise—
not knowing or caring what wisdom is?

Word feels like a thrown stone, with a stone
inside, and can't sit down to a good *Ham
Sah*, the world's oldest mantra, Word's new

shrink assures him: *you are that* in Sanskrit.
Exhale on *ham*; on *sah*, breathe in this world
Word never will get. A Sufi, on getting it,

goes all inspired, and dances, hymning a tune
luminous as the *ur*-terms of Word's two-year-old,
for whom *moon* is *moan, pain* is an airplane,

for whom stone turns to skin as light hits it.

IT IS NIGHT IN MY STUDY

after Miguel de Unamuno

It is night in my study.
Alone, I hear the steady
agitation in my chest, as if
thought had turned my heart to soot.
And I hear my blood
with its thrumming undercurrent
seep into my quiet study
the way water used to measure time
by filling the base of the water clock.
Here, at night, alone, this is my study,
the books mute. The lamp
rinses my sheet of paper with light.
All those who write, who meditate, or study—
their souls doze inside them;
and now, all around me, I can feel
some alert thing circling, once or twice,
a vagrant shadow among the other shadows.
Heart, soot, water, blood, clock. How many
years have passed since turning forty?
Here, alone, with no sound,
a single beguiling idea takes hold.
"When she wakes up, wondering
why I never came to bed,
she'll find my body here
still releasing its heat, turning white—

that thing I was, the person who waited
mute and still as a book,
light pouring out from the lamp."
I write one line, move to the next,
hoping they won't appear
like anybody's last testament
but instead, a letter, explicable
only to some,
lines taken down from the anxiety
of the shade's other side.
I'm finished, but I'm still alive.

Notes

The two adaptations of poems by Miguel de Unamuno take considerable liberties, deleting some passages from the originals and at times inventing lines.

"Queequeg's Ramadan" borrows some phrases from Chapter 17 of *Moby-Dick.*

"Singer" adapts and condenses Constance Hieatt's prose translation of "Deor" in *Beowulf and Other Old English Poems.*

Lines 21 and 22 of "Life and Death" come from George Gascoigne's "Lullaby of a Lover."

"Partial Glance, Through the *O.E.D.*'s Magnifying Glass, at 'Thing'" owes a debt to Robert Pinsky—who described at a poetry reading the Anglo-Saxon root of the word. Some of the poem's italicized passages adapt the *O.E.D.*'s historical examples of the word's usage. Albert Speer was Hitler's architect.

The first and last lines of "Starting and Ending with Sade"—as well as some details in quatrain three and the couplet—come from Francine Du Plessix Gray's *At Home with the Marquis de Sade.*

"Sixties Couple, the Haight" takes some liberties with a photograph included in *What Was True: The Photographs and Notebooks of William Gedney.* In the mid-sixties, the claim "Clapton is God" appeared on at least one brick wall in London. Nixon was elected in 1968 with the support of a so-called "silent majority."

The last line of "Late Quartet" derives from the first of the "Maxims and Arrows" in Nietzsche's *Twilight of the Gods.*

"After a Phrase by József" takes its first line from the poem "Attila József," included in *Attila József: Selected Poems and Texts,* translated by John Bátki.

The Author

Steven Cramer is the author of three previous poetry collections:
The Eye That Desires to Look Upward (1987), *The World Book* (1992), and
Dialogue for the Left and Right Hand (1997). His poems and criticism
have appeared in numerous literary journals, including *The Atlantic
Monthly, The Nation, The New Republic, The Paris Review, Partisan Review,
Poetry,* and *TriQuarterly;* as well as in *The POETRY Anthology,
1912–2002.* Recipient of fellowships from the Massachusetts
Artists Foundation and the National Endowment for the Arts, he
has taught literature and writing at Bennington College, Boston
University, M.I.T., Tufts University, and in the low-residency MFA
program at Queens University, Charlotte. He currently directs the
low-residency MFA program in creative writing at Lesley
University in Cambridge. He lives with his wife, Hilary, and their
two children, Charlotte and Ethan, in Lexington, Massachusetts.

Tad Dickenson